The Washington Monument

Lola Schaefer

Heinemann Library
Chicago, Illinois

© 2002 Reed Educational & Professional Publishing
Published by Heinemann Library,
an imprint of Reed Educational & Professional Publishing,
Chicago, IL

Customer Service 888-454-2279

Visit our website at www.heinemannlibrary.com

Designed by Depke Design
Printed and bound in China by South China Printing Company.

06 05
10 9 8 7 6 5 4 3 2

Library of Congress Cataloging-in-Publication Data
Schaefer, Lola M., 1950

    The Washington Monument / Lola M. Schaefer.

      p. cm. -- (Symbols of freedom)

    Includes bibliographical references (p.) and index

    ISBN 1-58810-179-7(HC), 1-58810-400-1(Pbk.)

      1. Washington Monument (Washington, D.C.)--Juvenile literature. 2. Washington (D.C.)--Buildings, structures, etc.--Juvenile literature. [1. Washington Monument (Washington, D.C.) 2. National monuments.] I. Title. II. Series.

F23.4.W3 S33 2001
975.3--dc21

                                        2001001634

Acknowledgments
The author and publishers are grateful to the following for permission to reproduce copyright material:
Cover photograph: Alan Schein/The Stock Market
pp. 5, 9 James P. Blair/Corbis; p. 6 Todd Gipstein/Corbis; pp. 7, 20, 21, 22, 23, 24, 25, 26 Corbis; p. 11 Ron Watts/Corbis; pp. 12, 13, 17, 27 Historical Society of Washington, D.C.; pp. 14, 16, 19 The Granger Collection, New York; p. 15 Kevin Fleming/Corbis; p. 28 AFP/Corbis;
p. 29 Dennis Cook/AP Photo; p. 30 Bob Rowan—Progressive Image/Corbis;

Every effort has been made to contact copyright holders of any material reproduced in this book.
Any omissions will be rectified in subsequent printings if notice is given to the publisher.

Some words are shown in bold, **like this.**
You can find out what they mean by looking
in the glossary.

Contents

The Washington Monument

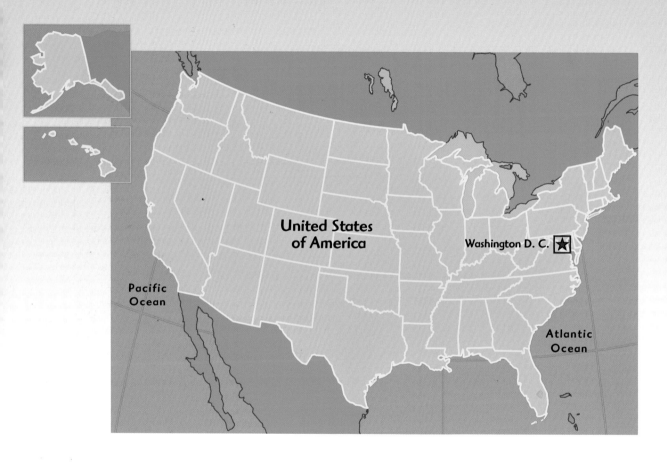

Alaska

Hawaii

United States of America

Washington D. C. ★

Pacific Ocean

Atlantic Ocean

The Washington **Monument** is one of the most famous buildings in the United States. It stands tall in Washington, D.C., the **capital** of the United States.

People from all over the world come to see
the Washington Monument. It is a **symbol**
that **honors** George Washington.

A Monument for the People

People have been visiting the Washington **Monument** for more than 100 years. Sometimes, large groups of people gather outside the monument to show how they feel about something.

Other times, people come to listen to music. Every Fourth of July, people watch fireworks at the Washington Monument. They celebrate our country's **independence**.

Visitors to the Monument

The Washington **Monument** is near the west end of the **National Mall**. This map shows the Washington Monument, the reflecting pool, and other **memorials** on the Mall.

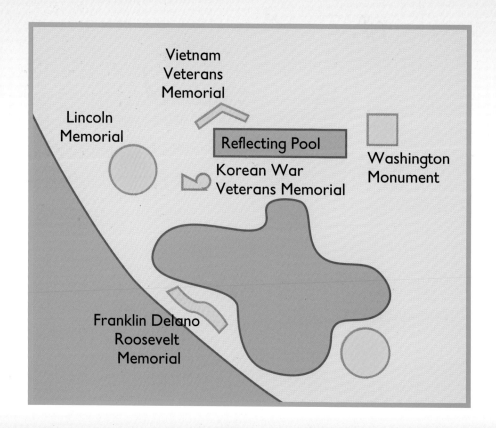

Vietnam Veterans Memorial

Lincoln Memorial

Reflecting Pool

Korean War Veterans Memorial

Washington Monument

Franklin Delano Roosevelt Memorial

More than 3,000 visitors tour the Washington Monument each day. **Park rangers** tell them about the monument and how it was built. The tour is free.

Outside the Monument

The Washington **Monument** is made of **marble**. It weighs as much as 15,000 African elephants.

The Washington Monument looks like a tall, pointed needle. It is as tall as 31 giraffes, one on top of another. People can see it from far away.

Inside the Monument

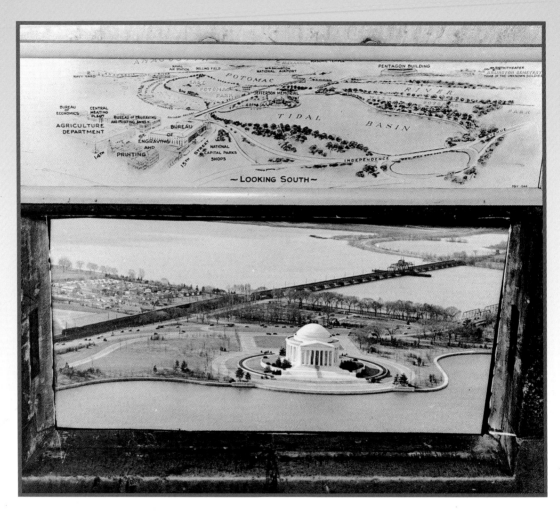

~ LOOKING SOUTH ~

Inside the Washington **Monument** there are 897 steps. But people ride in the elevator to get to the windows near the top. From there, they can see all around Washington, D.C.

Memorial stones line the stairway of the Washington Monument. All 193 stones **honor** George Washington. One stone honors the **stonemasons** who first worked on the monument.

13

George Washington

People built the Washington **Monument** to
remember George Washington. He was a
great leader during the **Revolutionary War**.
Later, he became the first president of the
United States.

At first, people wanted a statue of George
Washington. But plans changed, and work
began on the Washington Monument we
know today.

An Idea Is Born

Washington, D.C. was still a young city in 1833. A group of people formed the **Washington National Monument Society.** It was a kind of club that raised money to build the monument.

Later, the Society held a contest to find a **designer** for the monument. They chose Robert Mills. He drew a round building with statues. In the center there was a tall, pointed **obelisk**.

Work Begins

The United States **government** gave some land for the Washington **Monument** and park. On July 4, 1848, almost 20,000 people came to watch as the **cornerstone** was put in place.

For the next five years, **stonemasons** laid stone after stone. They made the **obelisk** taller. Soon, the monument stood as tall as a fifteen-story building.

Work Stops

There was an argument about who would be in charge of the Washington **Monument** project. Then the **designer,** Robert Mills, died. More and more people lost interest in the monument.

In 1861, the United States entered into the **Civil War.** Everyone was too busy with the war to think about the monument. For 25 years, work on the monument stopped.

New Life for the Monument

After the **Civil War**, the United States **government** put a new group of people in charge of the Washington **Monument** project. Some of them wanted the monument to have a whole new look.

Finally, everyone decided that the
monument should be just an **obelisk.**
The old **foundation** was made stronger,
so that it could hold up the heavy obelisk.

Work Begins Again

In the past, workers had used ropes and **pulleys** to lift the heavy stones. This time, they built an elevator inside the **monument**. It could do the heavy work.

They also placed a safety net outside the monument to catch workers if they fell. It worked! The net saved lives while the monument was built.

A Finishing Touch

The builders worried that the Washington **Monument** might be struck by lightning. When they put the **capstone** on, they put an **aluminum pyramid** on top.

26

On February 22, 1885, there was a ceremony
to celebrate the end of the work. President
Chester A. Arthur made a speech. It would
be three more years before the Washington
Monument was open to the public.

As Good as New

Over the years, the Washington **Monument** aged. Weather and visitors damaged the outside and inside. United States businesses and the **government** joined together to fix the monument.

From 1996 to 2000, workers fixed cracks and chips in the stone. They cleaned the inside walls. Today the monument is a safe place for all visitors.

Fact File

Washington Monument

★ Today, more than one million people ride the elevator each year to tour the Washington **Monument.**

★ Altogether, it took more than 100 years and 120 million dollars to complete the Washington Monument.

★ In 1848, a time capsule was placed in the **cornerstone** of the Washington Monument. It contained American coins, more than 50 newspapers, and information on the United States, Washington, D.C., and George Washington's family.

★ In 1884, **aluminum** was a rare and expensive metal. The aluminum **pyramid** that was put on top of the **capstone** cost $225. That was almost as much money as a worker earned in one year!

★ Before 1958, there were metal bars covering the windows at the top of the monument. The bars were replaced with safety glass to keep people from throwing things out the windows.

Glossary

aluminum light, sliver-colored metal that bends easily

capital important city where the government is located

capstone top stone

Civil War U.S. war in the 1800s, in which northern states fought against southern states

cornerstone first stone of a building that is going to be built

designer person who draws or plans something that could be built or made

foundation solid base on which a building is built

government people who rule or govern a country or state

honor to do something that shows great respect for someone or something

independence America's freedom from rule by Great Britain

marble hard, white stone used to make buildings and statues

memorial building or statue that helps us remember a person or idea

monument statue, stone, or building that helps us remember a person or idea

National Mall large area of land in Washington, D.C. where a museum, statues, and memorials are located

obelisk four-sided stone building that narrows to a triangle at the top

park ranger someone in charge of the park and the safety of visitors while at the park

pulley lifting machine made from a rope or chain and a set of grooved wheels

pyramid solid shape with a flat bottom and triangle-shaped sides that meet at a point on top

Revolutionary War war in which the thirteen American colonies won their freedom from Britain

stonemason someone who builds or works with stone

symbol something that stands for an idea

Washington National Monument Society group of people that began the organization and fund-raising for the Washington Monument

More Books to Read

An older reader can help you with these books.

Doherty, Craig. *The Washington Monument.* Woodbridge, Conn.: Blackbirch Press, 1995.

January, Brendan. *The National Mall.* Danbury, Conn.: Children's Press, 2000.

Schaefer, Lola M. *George Washington.* Mankato, Minn. Capstone Books, 1999.

Index